THE INDEPENDENT GUIDE TO THE UK CONSTITUTION

*By Andy McSmith, Will Gore, Oliver Wright,
James Cusick & Cahal Milmo*

Edited by Richard Askwith

Published by Independent Print Ltd
2 Derry Street, London W8 5HF

Table of Contents

THE INDEPENDENT / i GUIDE TO THE UK CONSTITUTION

THE WORD "constitution" sounds dry and academic. The subject is anything but. Many of the most explosive, life-changing themes of today's news agenda have their roots in the UK's often-praised but never-written-down constitution.

The relationship between Westminster and Brussels; the flaws in our voting system; the primacy – or otherwise – of British courts; the Union between England and the UK's other component parts; the proper role of the monarchy ... all these are issues with the potential to change fundamentally the character of British life.

If you want to understand what the arguments are, what the underlying facts are – or even what your individual rights are – you need to understand at least the basics of the UK's sometimes nebulous constitutional arrangements.

Based on the newspaper series with which "The Independent" and "i" have marked the 800th anniversary of Magna Carta, this book offers a simple, accessible overview of the current state of play in the most important constitutional areas. It also includes extracts from, and summaries of, some of the key texts that, in the absence of a written constitution, are the closest thing there is to a codification of the ground rules of British democracy.

The UK's democratic liberties are the envy of the world. They are also precarious. We have no written constitution, and the unwritten traditions on which we rely instead are increasingly being called into question. They are an imperfect guarantee of our freedoms, but they are best we have. Unless we value and understand them, those freedoms could all too easily be lost.

We hope this book will prove a helpful starting-point for those who wish to learn more about this crucial aspect of modern life.

THE RIGHTS OF CITIZENS

ANDY McSMITH reflects on the 800-year-old precedent of Magna Carta – and what it tells us about a subject of vital national importance

=

A FURIOUS political row over human rights is on the boil. It is not about what those rights should be but over who makes the decision, whether the final arbitrator of the rights of a British citizen should be the British government, or a European court.

When David Cameron agreed to include in the Conservative election manifesto a promise to repeal the 1998 Human Rights Act, he may have calculated that he would be denied a majority in the Commons and provided therefore with a cast iron alibi for dropping the whole idea.

As it is, the newly appointed Justice Secretary, Michael Gove, has no choice but to draw up a British Bill of Rights – something no previous Lord Chancellor has done in the many centuries during which that office has existed – and place it before Parliament to see if the votes are there to get it through. What set this off was a ruling from the European Court of Justice that prisoners in British jails should have the right to vote. Since this is where it all began, it might reasonably be assumed that the purpose of the new act will be to remove rights that people have under European law which the government thinks they should not have, rather than to give any British citizens any new rights.

This then throws up a major complication, because the UK is a signatory of the European Convention on

Human Rights. Indeed, the UK and France were the two nations, more than any others, that created the ECHR. The convention is separate from the EU. Created in 1953, it is also older than the EU, and covers every country in Europe except Belarus – including, for instance, Russia, where that brave minority fighting for human rights see it as a valuable safeguard.

If the UK withdrew from the Convention, the effect could reverberate across Europe. Yet if we remain within the ECHR – which is apparently what David Cameron and Michael Gove intend – the possibility remains that someone who thinks that their unalienable rights have been denied by the British courts could still appeal to the European Court over the heads of Britain's judges. That would then raise the question of whether there was any point to passing a new human rights act at all.

It is up to the Conservatives to sort out the politics of all this. What matters more to most of us is the deeper question of what our "unalienable rights" are, and whether the law will continue to protect them. This is a question on which most people have a clear and broadly accurate general idea, while being hazy about where these rights originate.

Anyone who does not already know that the Magna Carta was "signed" (when King John placed his royal seal on the document) 800 years ago this month will doubtless be reminded by the celebrations surrounding the anniversary (on 15 June), and will know that in some unspecified way our ancient rights as British citizens spring from that document. But how?

Most educated people in the English speaking world have also heard the famous passage from the 1776 American Declaration of Independence, which was indirectly influenced by Magna Carta. It says: "We hold these truths to be self-evident, that all men are created equal, that they are endowed by their Creator with certain un-alienable rights, that among these are Life, Liberty and the pursuit of Happiness..."

Actually, these truths are not "self-evident". They are not evident at all, for instance, in North Korea, or in parts of the world ruled by religious zealots. When Thomas Jefferson wrote them, he was being deliberately provocative, throwing those words in the face of the British property-owning class who believed that they had a right to hold arbitrary power in check, but did not extend that right to American colonists. Jefferson him-self, despite his proclaimed belief in an "unalienable right" to liberty, was a slave-owner.

Yet the fact remains that, in our liberal democracy, we do believe that citizens have unalienable rights – and not just those listed by Thomas Jefferson. Most people in modern Britain would say that a UK citizen has a right to free speech, a right to express their sexuality, a right to belong to any legal organisation he or she chooses to belong to, a right to be paid if he or she is in work; some might add to these a right also to have paid work, and a right to eat, to be housed, to be educated, and to be cared for when old or sick. But the legal document that defines all these rights does not exist. They are certainly not found in Magna Carta, which lists all sorts of stric-tures that mean absolutely nothing to us – such as "heirs may be given in marriage, but not to someone of lower social standing"; or: "no town or person shall be forced to build bridges over rivers except those with an ancient obligation to do so."

There is just one section that has resonated through the ages, way down the text in clauses 39 and 40, which say that "no free man shall be seized or imprisoned, or stripped of his rights or possessions, or outlawed or ex-iled, or deprived of his standing in any way, nor will we proceed with force against him, or send others to do so, except by the lawful judgment of his equals or by the law of the land" and "to no one will we sell, to no one deny or delay right or justice."

Magna Carta's purpose was to protect the barons, and to some extent all England's free men – but not the women, nor the serfs who made up most of the population – from arbitrary rule by a weak, tyrannical king. Its importance is that it set down in writing that there were circumstances in which even the king was subject to the law; and that it was recognised by subsequent kings.

When people refer to the "British constitution", they do not mean Magna Carta. Instead there is what is known as the "body of law" – the combined total of Acts of Parliament and judgments reached in court cases, which are scattered over countless law books and statutes. None of these has the weight of a constitution in itself; yet taken together they carry too much weight to be easily set aside.

One of the first serious attempts to collect and codify all these judgments, and so give England a written body of constitutional law, was made in the 1760s by the jurist William Blackstone, whose four volumes of Commentaries were read avidly by the USA's founding fathers.

Some of what Blackstone wrote sounds weird to the modern ear (for example, his assertion that kings could do no wrong); and there have been other heavyweight codifiers since – AV Dicey, Walter Bagehot, even Sir Gus O'Donnell – who are arguably equally significant as authors of what passes for the UK's written constitution.

Yet it was Blackstone who wrote one powerful sentence that neatly disposed of the idea that any idea of what is good for the public as a whole should ever be a pretext for trampling on individual human rights. "The public good," he wrote, "is in nothing more essentially interested, than in the protection of every individual's private rights."

This collection of articles marks the 800th anniversary of Magna Carta's signing by reviewing the written foundations, such as they are, to what passes for the UK constitution. The series offers a guide not just to the main points of that constitution but also to the documents in which those points can be found. These are big issues. Yet it is arguable that all that matters in our constitution is expressed in that single sentence of Blackstone. It is on its underlying assumption – that an individual citizen's rights are so important than they take primacy over religious zeal or government policy – that liberal democracy is built.

OUR UNWRITTEN CONSTITUTION

20 KEY TEXTS

Throughout this collection, we will quote from and refer to some of the many texts - statutes, declarations, legal judgments and learned works – which together provide some of the written underpinning for the UK's constitutional arrangements. References to the following, in particular, are likely to become familiar...

1 | 'MAGNA CARTA' (1215)

Signed by King John on 15 June 1215, the first Magna Carta is now of largely symbolic value. But paragraphs 39 and 40 remain the most famous of all assertions of British subjects' rights.

2 | ASSIZE OF CLARENDON (1166)

Promulgated by Henry II, this otherwise obscure document is the earliest significant written underpinning of the principle of trial by jury.

3 | PETITION OF RIGHT (1628)

The document that provoked Charles I into ruling for 11 years without Parliament, this is a fundamental assertion of those rights of the subject that cannot be usurped by the monarch.

4 | HABEAS CORPUS ACT (1679)

Prohibits the indefinite detention of suspects without trial.

5 | BILL OF RIGHTS (1689)

The legislative fruit of the Glorious Revolution of 1688, this crucial document lays down limits on the powers of the monarch and sets out the rights of Parliament.

6 | ACT OF SETTLEMENT (1701)

Guarantees the independence of the judiciary from royal interference.

7 | 'COMMENTARIES ON THE LAWS OF ENGLAND', BY SIR WILLIAM BLACKSTONE (1765-1769)

The first serious attempt to codify the countless legal judgments and statutes relating to constitutional issues.

8 | 'THE ENGLISH CONSTITUTION', BY WALTER BAGEHOT (1867 & 1873)

Another commentary that has acquired semi-institutional status. Particularly good on defining the largely indefinable role of the Monarch in relation to Parliament.

9 | 'A PRACTICAL TREATISE ON THE LAW, PRIVILEGES, PROCEEDINGS AND USAGE OF PARLIAMENT', BY ERSKINE MAY (1844)

Still being updated; often cited as the ultimate authority on parliamentary procedure and the relationships between the executive, the legislature and the sovereign.

10 | 'AN INTRODUCTION TO THE STUDY OF THE LAW OF THE CONSTITUTION', BY A V DICEY (1885)

Source of the oft-quoted view that the "twin pillars" of the UK constitution are the supremacy of Parliament and the "rule of law".

11 | THE PARLIAMENT ACT (1911)

Limits the power of the House of Lords to block legislation passed by the Commons.

12 | THE SALISBURY CONVENTION (1945)

Established the principle that peers in the House of Lords should not oppose legislation that appeared in the governing party's election manifesto once it reaches its second reading.

13 | *THE EUROPEAN COMMUNITIES ACT (1972)*
The legal basis (with various successor acts and treaties) of the UK's membership of the EU. Declares that all present or future "rights, liabilities, obligations and restrictions" created by European law will automatically be applicable in the UK, "without further enactment" by Parliament.

14 | *LAWS IN WALES ACTS (1536 AND 1543)*
Now superseded, this legislation remains significant for its unambiguous assertion that Wales is "for ever from henceforth incorporated, united and annexed to" England.

15 | *THE ACTS OF UNION (1707, 1800 AND 1801)*
The 1707 Act decreed that "England and Scotland be forever united in one kingdom by the name of Great Britain". The 1800 and 1801 Acts created a single polity of Great Britain and Ireland.

16 | *THE SCOTLAND ACT (1998), THE NORTHERN IRELAND ACT (1998) AND THE GOVERNMENT OF WALES ACTS (1998 & 2006)*
Established the three devolved legislatures which exist today.

17 | *HUMAN RIGHTS ACT (1998)*
Defines the relationship between UK statute and the European Convention of
Human Rights; includes a rare statutory statement of the right to freedom of speech.

18 | *R (SIMMS) V HOME SECRETARY (1999)*
Lord Hoffmann's judgment laid down the principle that: Parliamentary sovereignty means Parliament can, if it

chooses, legislate contrary to fundamental principles of human rights.

19 | THE CONSTITUTIONAL REFORM ACT (2005)
Modified the office of the Lord Chancellor and set up a Supreme Court; also created an independent Judicial Appointments Commission – removing the monarch's role in the appointment of judges.

20 | CABINET MANUAL (2011)
The most up-to-date document setting out the laws, conventions and rules setting out how Government works, with particular reference to the formation of governments.

OUR TROUBLED JOURNEY TO AN INDEPENDENT JUDICIARY

WILL GORE describes the vital importance – and painful evolution – of the principle of the separation of powers

=

IN POPULAR perception the Middle Ages was a time of lawlessness and cruelty. And to a degree, that characterisation holds true. Crusades abroad, ill-disciplined governance at home, England in the early thirteenth century was not exactly enlightened.

The creation of Magna Carta in 1215 is all the more remarkable against such a backdrop. An unpopular king brought to heel by a written agreement sounds much too good to be true – and it was, in the short-term, with peaceable discussions giving way to civil war within a matter of months.

Nevertheless, the legacy of the charter signed by King John and the barons at Runnymede 800 years ago has been compelling, both in this country and beyond. The original agreement may not have protected rights and freedoms in the detailed way which modern-day myth occasionally suggests, but it undoubtedly set Britain on a road towards non-autocratic government.

In particular, Magna Carta achieved acceptance for two key principles. The first was that regal authority should be limited by – and separated from – the will of the people. In the immediate context of the early 1200s, that meant that taxes could not be raised without the "general consent of the realm" – and for realm read barons and the church. Even so, as a guiding principle, it

14

was crucial.

The second fundamental doctrine was that individuals were entitled to be treated in accordance with the laws of the land and would, when accused of wrongdoing, be judged by their equals. Again, the contemporary impact of this element of Magna Carta – the famed clause 39 – was limited to the minority of British citizens who were "free men". However, it confirmed the notion of the rule of law and the applicability of trial by jury, which had seen its origins during Henry II's rule in the previous century when the first judges emerged too.

Ultimately, then, Magna Carta was a bulwark against tyranny. For thirteenth century barons it was also a tool for the advance of oligarchy, a means of protecting their role as the advisors to the king – their positions as such having been established informally during the reign of William the Conqueror. Magna Carta certainly did not envisage genuine democratic rights as they are understood today.

Indeed, the continuing acceptance of a formalised and symbiotic relationship between the monarch and his (important) subjects was not without its hiccups – to put things mildly. And the development of regular parliaments in the mid- to late-thirteenth century (and especially their extension to include non-noble representatives) was largely the consequence of discord, rather than harmonious reform.

The security of parliament's role – separated into two chambers from the mid-14th century – and the independence of the judiciary were largely dependent on the strength or weakness of successive monarchs. Henry VIII's "great matter" and the subsequent break from Rome have been seen by many historians as the point at which parliamentary power took on a new character, although Tudor monarchs were canny enough to recognise that empowering parliament was a means to legit-imising their own authority. Fundamentally, though, the monarch retained a firm grip on the power of the execu-tive veto.

But if the Tudor period, rumbustious as it was, wit-nessed a new understanding of the need for balance in the relationship between executive, legislature and judi-ciary, so it was the dramatic failure of the Stuart kings to accept the limitations of their power which ultimately led to the more formal separation of the three arms of state.

The Star Chamber was originally conceived as a kind of supervisory body to oversee the operation of Eng-land's lower courts and consider appeals, as well as to ensure enforcement of the law against those powerful enough to avoid the clutches of local judicial officials. Yet under James I, the Chamber effectively became the king's private enforcement agency, meting out judg-ments on moral as well as legal matters. The court was used to suppress dissent and to bypass the necessity of calling parliaments.

The dismissal by James I of Edward Coke, the Chief Justice, for having suggested that the king was subject to the law, rather than the other way round, brought mat-ters to a head. Incensed, Coke dedicated himself to writ-ing The Institutes of the Lawes of England, which em-phasised the role of Magna Carta as the basis for the common law and, notably, as having enshrined the in-dependence of the judiciary from monarchical control. Coke subsequently drafted The Petition of Right, an up-dated Magna Carta, which parliament compelled the new king, Charles I, unhappily to accept. Charles re-sponded by governing without parliament for 11 years and ramping up his persecution of those who opposed him. The English Civil War, which followed, ended with

Charles' execution, convicted by a jury of 120 officials of the highest rank available.

Coke's assertion of Magna Carta's formative place in English constitutional history, especially in confirming the independence of the judiciary, has been upheld with remarkable consistency throughout the last 350 years. The Glorious Revolution of 1688 and the subsequent passage of the Bill of Rights, followed a decade later by the Act of Settlement, finally – and for good – ended any pretensions that a monarch might have to absolute rule and cemented the separate functions of crown, parliament and courts.

In recent decades, constitutional changes have further reinforced the separation of state powers (even if the continued existence of the executive within the legislature raises theoretical difficulties). The last Labour government, for instance, ended the legal function of the House of Lords, transferring power to the Supreme Court as the UK's highest legal authority, and provided for more independence in the appointment of judges.

Yet it is the great irony of Britain's unwritten constitution that having arguably reached a point of greatest clarity, so it is up for renewed debate. The role of the European Convention on Human Rights, as legislated for by the Human Rights Act here; the existence of the Strasbourg court; clashes between ministers and judicial officials over their respective roles; and ongoing questions over House of Lords reform – not to mention the state of the Union between Scotland and England: all have become major talking points. Magna Carta, which was intended to resolve a specific set of contemporary problems in 1215, has come for many to represent a simpler, more English, representation of rights.

In the final analysis, however, it is the incremental reforms which have taken place in the last 800 years that are the hallmark of British government and governance. To ignore that is to disregard the struggles of those who have endeavoured to ensure respect for the rule of law and to maintain the delicate balance between the powers that rule our lives.

OUR UNWRITTEN CONSTITUTION

KEY TEXTS ON THE RULE OF LAW

A | FROM MAGNA CARTA (1215) (PARAGRAPHS 39, 40 AND 45)
39: ...No freemen shall be taken or imprisoned or disseised or exiled or in any way destroyed, nor will we go upon him nor send upon him, except by the lawful judgment of his peers or by the law of the land.
40: To no one will we sell, to no one will we refuse or delay, right or justice...
45: We will appoint as justices, constables, sheriffs, or bailiffs only such as know the law of the realm and mean to observe it well.

B | FROM THE ASSIZE OF CLARENDON (1166) (PARAGRAPH 1)
1: ...The said King Henry ordained... that inquiry be made through the several counties and through the several hundreds by twelve more lawful men of the hundred and by four more lawful men of each vill, upon oath that they will tell the truth, whether in their hundred or in their vill there is any man cited or charged as himself being a robber or murderer or thief...

C | FROM 'COMMENTARIES ON THE LAWS OF ENGLAND' (1765) BY SIR WILLIAM BLACKSTONE, BOOK 1, CHAPTER 1
[This land is]... a land... in which political or civil liberty is the very end and scope of the constitution. This liberty, rightly understood, consists in the power of doing whatever the laws permit; which is only to be effected by a general conformity of all orders and degrees to those equitable rules of action, by which the meanest

individual is protected from the insults and oppression of the greatest...

D | *FROM THE PETITION OF RIGHT (1628) (PARAGRAPH 10)*

...that no man hereafter be compelled to make or yield any gift, loan, benevolence, tax, or such like charge, without common consent by act of parliament; and that none be called to make answer, or take such oath, or to give attendance, or be confined, or otherwise molested or disquieted concerning the same or for refusal thereof; and that no freeman, in any such manner as is before mentioned, be imprisoned or detained...

E | *FROM THE BILL OF RIGHTS (1689)*

[The] Lords Spiritual and Temporal and Commons... being now assembled in a full and free representative of this nation... do in the first place (as their ancestors in like case have usually done) for the vindicating and asserting their ancient rights and liberties declare: that the pretended power of suspending the laws or the execution of laws by regal authority without consent of Parliament is illegal; that the pretended power of dispensing with laws or the execution of laws by regal authority, as it hath been assumed and exercised of late, is illegal; ...that levying money for or to the use of the Crown by pretence of prerogative, without grant of Parliament, for longer time, or in other manner than the same is or shall be granted, is illegal; that it is the right of the subjects to petition the king...; that the raising or keeping a standing army within the kingdom in time of peace, unless it be with consent of Parliament, is against law; ...that election of members of Parliament ought to be free; that the freedom of speech and debates or proceedings in Parliament ought not to be impeached or questioned in any court or place out of Parliament; that excessive bail ought not to be required, nor excessive fines imposed, nor cruel and unusual punishments inflicted; ...and that for redress of all grievances, and for the amending, strengthening and preserving of the laws, Parliaments ought to be held frequently.

F | FROM THE CONSTITUTIONAL REFORM ACT (2005) (PART 2, SECTION 3)

(1) The Lord Chancellor, other Ministers of the Crown and all with responsibility for matters relating to the judiciary or otherwise to the administration of justice must uphold the continued independence of the judiciary.

(2) Subsection (1) does not impose any duty which it would be within the legislative competence of the Scottish Parliament to impose.

(3) A person is not subject to the duty imposed by subsection (1) if he is subject to the duty imposed by section 1(1) of the Justice (Northern Ireland) Act 2002 (c. 26).

(4) The following particular duties are imposed for the purpose of upholding that independence.

(5) The Lord Chancellor and other Ministers of the Crown must not seek to influence particular judicial decisions through any special access to the judiciary.

(6) The Lord Chancellor must have regard to:

(a) the need to defend
that independence;

(b) the need for the judiciary to have the support necessary to enable them to exercise their functions;

(c) the need for the public interest in regard to matters relating to the judiciary or otherwise to the administration of justice to be properly represented in decisions affecting those matters.

(7) In this section "the judiciary" includes the judiciary of any of the following:

(a) the Supreme Court;
(b) any other court established under the law of any part of the United Kingdom;
(c) any international court.
(8) In subsection (7) "international court" means the International Court of Justice or any other court or tribunal which exercises jurisdiction, or performs functions of a judicial nature, in pursuance of:
(a) an agreement to which the United Kingdom or Her Majesty's Government in the United Kingdom is a party, or (b) a resolution of the Security Council or General Assembly of the United Nations.

G | FROM THE CONSTITUTIONAL REFORM ACT (2005) (PART 3, SECTION 23)
(1) There is to be a Supreme Court of the United Kingdom.
(2) The Court consists of 12 judges appointed by Her Majesty by letters patent.
(3) Her Majesty may from time to time by Order in Council amend subsection (2) so as to increase or further increase the number of judges of the Court.
(4) No recommendation may be made to Her Majesty in Council to make an Order under subsection (3) unless a draft of the Order has been laid before and approved by resolution of each House of Parliament.
(5) Her Majesty may by letters patent appoint one of the judges to be President and
one to be Deputy President of the Court.
(6) The judges other than the President and Deputy President are to be styled "Justices of the Supreme Court".
(7) The Court is to be taken to be duly constituted despite any vacancy among the judges of the Court or in the office of President or Deputy President.

THE PEOPLE'S MANDATE: HOW IS THE RIGHT TO GOVERN CONFERRED?

ANDY McSMITH explains the largely informal rules that determine who has the right to form a government

=

IF THE opinion polls published before this year's general election had turned out to be accurate, we might still be without a government. In 2010, it took five frantic days to form a coalition after the Conservatives failed to win an overall majority in the House of Commons. It was always clear, though, that the governing party would be the one that reached an agreement with the Liberal Democrats, and it was always more likely to be the Conservatives than Labour.

This year, we were led to expect a more confused picture, with the SNP as the third party and the Liberal Democrats reduced to a rump, so that it might have been necessary for three or even four political parties to strike up a deal before anyone could claim to have a working majority.

In the end, this was all academic. Unless there is some major convulsion inside the Conservative Party, or a long string of by-election defeats, they are securely in office until May 2020. That date is fixed because the one major constitutional change which the Coalition government got on to the statute books was the Fixed Term Parliament Act (2011), which decrees that unless there is a major crisis, there will always be five years between one general election and the next. For the previous 100 years, that figure of five years was the maximum time permitted by law, but within that time an election took place when the prime minister chose to call it – unless the government was brought down by a vote of no confidence, in which case the prime minister had no choice but to go to the country.

Forming a government after an election may look simple enough in the UK. This is because, as events have worked out, every general election since the war – except those of February 1974 and 2010 – has produced an outright majority for either the Conservatives or Labour. Even in those, two, exceptional cases, the question of who governed was quickly resolved.

But the public willingness to keep on voting for the big parties is diminishing. This year's result was notable for the impressive gains in the votes cast for the SNP, Ukip and the Greens – though only the geographically-concentrated SNP had the MPs to show for it. It may well be that next time the public will deliver a dramatic "plague on both your houses" message to the Conservatives and Labour, throwing up a messy result from which it really is not clear at all who has the right to be prime minister.

In this tricky situation, it is theoretically up to the monarch to appoint a prime minister – but only in theory. The last monarch who actually chose a prime minister to suit his prejudices was William IV, in 1834. He did not like the way the Whigs were reforming the system, sacked the Prime Minister, Lord Melbourne, and sent for the Tory leader, Sir Robert Peel, But Peel could not command a majority in the Commons, and was forced to hold an election, which he lost, putting Melbourne back in office, making the king look foolish. Since then, it has been agreed on all sides that monarchs should stay out of party politics.

But suppose that next time there were two contenders, each claiming to be the rightful prime minister, neither being prepared to give way to the other. How then could the monarch stay neutral? Such a situation did in fact arise, in February 1974, when the Conservatives won more votes than Labour, but Labour won more seats. Under those circumstances, according to the manual that the former Cabinet Secretary Sir Gus O'Donnell compiled at Gordon Brown's request, the responsibility of advising the monarch "falls especially on the incumbent Prime Minister, who at the time of his or her resignation may also be asked by the Sovereign for a recommendation on who can best command the confidence of the House of Commons in his or her place."

During those five days in 2010 when Gordon Brown was still in No 10, he was unfairly accused of clinging to office after being rejected by the electors – when in fact he was doing what the Cabinet manual required him to do. He actually accepted defeat gracefully once he knew that Nick Clegg had struck a deal with David Cameron. Edward Heath was also accused of clinging on too long in 1974, but he, too, was within his rights to do so. No matter how messy the result of the 2020 election, the one certainty is that on the Friday morning after polling day, the Conservative incumbent would still be Prime Minister, and the more complicated the situation was, the longer he or she would be likely to continue squatting in Downing Street.

Even when the dust settled, what remained might well not be the kind of stable coalition that came into being in 2010. It is possible for a minority party to govern without a majority in the House of Commons, which has happened for short periods since 1945. Such a government may not be able to do much, but so long as it can get a budget passed every year and not lose a confidence vote – as the minority Labour government in 1979 eventually did – it can muddle on. This can be done through what is called a "confidence and supply" arrangement, under which the minor party agrees not to support a no confidence vote and not to vote down the Queen's Speech or a Budget. The House of Lords is not involved in these arrangements. Even in Victorian times, Tory aristocrats such as Lord Salisbury, who was Prime Minister from 1895 to 1902, realised that there had to be a limit to how far unelected peers could thwart an elected government. He devised the unwritten Salisbury Convention, which is now interpreted as meaning that the Lords will never try to vote down a measure that was included in the ruling party's election manifesto.

There was a crisis in 1910 when the Conservative majority in the House of Lords blocked the Liberal government's budget. This led to the Parliament Act (1911), which took the budget out of the hands of the upper house altogether, and laid down that peers could amend and hold up legislation passed by the Commons, but not ultimately block it. The Act also shortened the maximum time between general elections from seven years to five. In 1949, the Labour government introduced another act which shortened the maximum time over which the lords could block legislation. So, no matter how complicated the business of forming a government, those involved can take comfort in the thought that, once it is sorted in the House of Commons, the job is done.

OUR UNWRITTEN CONSTITUTION

KEY TEXTS ON THE FORMATION OF GOVERNMENTS

A | FROM THE CABINET MANUAL (2011; '2: ELECTIONS AND GOVERNMENT FORMATION')

"... 2.8 Prime Ministers hold office unless and until they resign. If the Prime Minister resigns on behalf of the Government, the Sovereign will invite the person who appears most likely to be able to command the confidence of the House to serve as Prime Minister and to form a government.

... 2.11 After an election, if an incumbent government retains an overall majority ... it will normally continue in office and resume normal business. There is no need for the Sovereign to ask the Prime Minister to continue. If the election results in an overall majority for a different party, the incumbent Prime Minister and government will immediately resign and the Sovereign will invite the leader of the party that has won the election to form a government...

... 2.12 Where an election does not result in an overall majority for a single party, the incumbent government remains in office unless and until the Prime Minister tenders his or her resignation and the Government's resignation to the Sovereign. An incumbent government is entitled to wait until the new Parliament has met to see if it can command the confidence of the House of Commons, but is expected to resign if it becomes clear that it is unlikely to be able to command that confidence and there is a clear alternative.

... 2.18 Where a Prime Minister chooses to resign from his or her individual position at a time when his or her administration has an overall majority in the House of Commons, it is for the party or parties in government to identify who can be chosen as the successor...

... 2.19 ...If a government is defeated on a motion that 'this House has no confidence in Her Majesty's Government', there is then a 14-day period during which an alternative government can be formed from the House of Commons as presently constituted, or the incumbent government can seek to regain the confidence of the House. If no government can secure the confidence of the House of Commons during that period, through the approval of a motion that 'this House has confidence in Her Majesty's Government', a general election will take place..."

B | FROM THE FIXED TERM PARLIAMENTS ACT (2011)
"1 (3) The polling day for each subsequent parliamentary general election is to be the first Thursday in May in the fifth calendar year following that in which the polling day for the previous parliamentary general election fell....

... 2 (1) An early parliamentary general election is to take place if –

(a) the House of Commons passes a motion in the form set out in subsection (2), and

(b) if the motion is passed on a division, the number of members who vote in favour of the motion is a number equal to or greater than two thirds of the number of seats in the House (including vacant seats).

(2) The form of motion for the purposes of subsection (1)(a) is – "That there shall be an early parliamentary general election."

(3) An early parliamentary general election is also to take place if –

(a) the House of Commons passes a motion in the form set out in subsection (4), and

(b) the period of 14 days after the day on which that motion is passed ends without the House passing a mo-

28

tion in the form set out in subsection (5).

(4) The form of motion for the purposes of subsection (3)(a) is – "That this House has no confidence in Her Majesty's Government."

(5) The form of motion for the purposes of subsection (3)(b) is – "That this House has confidence in Her Majesty's Government."

C | FROM THE ENGLISH CONSTITUTION, BY WALTER BAGEHOT (2ND EDITION, 1873; '1: THE CABINET')

"As a rule, the nominal Prime Minister is chosen by the legislature, and the real Prime Minister for most purposes – the leader of the House of Commons – almost without exception so. There is nearly always some one man plainly selected by the voice of the predominant party in the predominant house of the legislature to head that party, and consequently to rule the nation. We have in England an elective first magistrate as truly as the Americans have an elective first magistrate. The Queen is only at the head of the dignified part of the Constitution. The Prime Minister is at the head of the efficient part. The Crown is, according to the saying, the 'fountain of honour'; but the Treasury is the spring of business. Nevertheless, our first magistrate differs from the American. He is not elected directly by the people; he is elected by the representatives of the people. He is an example of 'double election'. The legislature chosen, in name, to make laws, in fact finds its principle business in making and keeping an executive."

D | FROM ERSKINE MAY'S PARLIAMENTARY PRACTICE (24TH EDITION, 2011)

"From time to time the Opposition put down a motion on the paper expressing lack of confidence in the Government or otherwise criticising its general conduct. By established convention the Government always accedes

to the demand from the Leader of the Opposition to al-
lot a day for the discussion of a motion tabled by the official Opposition which, in the Government's view,
would have the effect of testing the confidence of the
House. In allotting a day for this purpose the Government is entitled to have regard to the exigencies of its
own business, but a reasonably early day is invariably
found. This convention is founded on the recognised position of the Opposition as a potential Government,
which guarantees the legitimacy of such an interruption
of the normal course of business."

WHERE POWER RESIDES: THE SIMPLE RULE THAT TRUMPS EVERYTHING

OLIVER WRIGHT reflects on a vital principle of sovereignty

=

LOOKING AROUND at the faces of new MPs, wandering bemused, around the Houses of Parliament over the past few weeks, it is easy to forget just what extraordinary power these individuals now hold.

As humble new backbenchers they may not think so, but it is no exaggeration to say that collectively and constitutionally they are now members of an institution that is nothing short of an elected dictatorship. In the general humdrum reality of British political life these powers may be theoretical – but no one living in this country should be under any doubt that they are there.

Take just a few examples. Parliament alone can determine what is legal and what is illegal in Britain – as well as the punishment for illegality. It can make war. It can dispatch ministers; prime ministers; even kings and queens. A simple majority vote in Parliament would be enough to bring back the death penalty; abolish the BBC; withdraw from the European Union; hand over the Isle of Wight to Russia; or unleash Britain's nuclear weapons.

When it is said that Parliament is "sovereign" it means just that. Over hundreds of years – through wars, negotiations, executions and conventions – it has amassed all the powers of the state that used to be in

31

the hands of absolute medieval sovereignty. As the Swiss political theorist Jean-Louis de Lolme put it in his – not uncritical – 1771 book on the English constitution: "Parliament can do everything but make a woman a man and a man a woman." Even that is now a moot point, given recent medical advances.

In reality, of course, how Parliament exercises its power is constrained by myriad "real-life" factors. But the fact remains that, in theory at least, our 650 elected MPs and 800-odd unelected peers have far more power than most of us who voted for them would ever imagine.

The basic reason for this is that, unlike other countries – notably the United States – we do not have a written constitution whose broad principles of citizens' rights and responsibilities trump the will of the elected assembly.

In the US, Congress can pass laws, but it is ultimately the Supreme Court that judges whether those laws are "constitutional". In Britain we have a Supreme Court, but it can only interpret the laws as laid down by Parliament and the treaties that Parliament has signed up to. If the Supreme Court rules something is illegal, a simple majority vote in Parliament can make it legal.

And that is very significant. Take, for example, the bête noire of the Conservative right: the power of the European Court of Human Rights over British law. In reality the European Court has constitutional authority over our laws only because Parliament has agreed to it. If a future parliament (or indeed government) were to withdraw from the Convention on Human Rights, the court would have no authority over the UK whatsoever.

The same is true of the European Union. The UK courts recognise the supremacy of EU law on those subjects where the EU can legislate. However, this supremacy derives from the European Communities Act 1972 (and its successor acts), which could be repealed by a future parliament.

So what does sovereignty actually mean? How did the concept develop? And what is the relationship between the two elements of Parliament: the Commons and the Lords?

Sovereignty means that Parliament can make laws concerning anything. It means that no Parliament can "bind" a future parliament to something on which it has previously legislated; and that a valid Act of Parliament cannot be questioned by a court of law.

The root of these powers goes back to the English Civil War but it was not until the Glorious Revolution and the Bill of Rights (1689) that stemmed from it that the concept of parliamentary sovereignty really took root.

That document, for the first time, laid down limits on the powers of the monarch and set out the rights of Parliament, including the requirement for regular parliaments, free elections, and freedom of speech in Parliament. It also stated that no laws could be dispensed with or suspended without the consent of Parliament and that no taxes could be levied without its authority.

Since then, parliamentary power has evolved without recourse to another such fundamental document of rights. Powers that used to be the preserve of the sovereign have gradually been transferred to Parliament while the Commons has exerted its supremacy over the Lords. For example, the Parliament Act 1911 abolished the power of the House of Lords to veto a bill passed by the House of Commons (peers can now delay legislation only for a defined period of time). Similarly, in 1945, faced with the prospect of a Labour-dominated Commons and a Conservative-dominated Lords, the leaders of both Houses agreed the Salisbury Convention: that is, that in future, peers should not oppose legislation contained in a party's election manifesto at second reading. It is, however, no more than a convention.

But while Britain does not have a written constitution defining the powers of Parliament it is not entirely true to say that none of the UK constitution's rules is written down. In fact, there are several documents that come close to being constitutional textbooks.

The most important of these (which is still updated more than 170 years after publication) is Erskine May's A Treatise upon the Law, Privileges, Proceedings and Usage of Parliament. This sets down the rules of parliamentary procedure and the relationship between the executive, legislature and sovereign and is still regularly cited as the ultimate arbiter of Britain's unwritten constitution.

Yet the truth is it is only a guide; and the principal point remains. Britain's system of government has been built up over the years on foundations that consist largely of convention, with no overarching legal document that codifies and guarantees the rights of citizens. As long as that remains the case – and repeated calls for a constitutional convention to rectify the situation show little sign of being heeded – the theoretical power of Parliament is fundamentally unchecked.

OUR UNWRITTEN CONSTITUTION

KEY TEXTS ON THE SOVEREIGNTY OF PARLIAMENT

A | FROM THE PETITION OF RIGHT (1628)

"To the King's Most Excellent Majesty... your subjects have inherited this freedom, that they should not be compelled to contribute to any tax, tallage, aid, or other like charge not set by common consent, in parliament."

B | FROM THE BILL OF RIGHTS (1689)

"The... Lords Spiritual and Temporal and Commons... being now assembled in a full and free representative of this nation... do in the first place (as their ancestors in like case have usually done) for the vindicating and asserting their ancient rights and liberties declare:

• That the pretended power of suspending the laws or the execution of laws by regal authority without consent of Parliament is illegal;

• That the pretended power of dispensing with laws or the execution of laws by regal authority, as it hath been assumed and exercised of late, is illegal;

• That levying money for or to the use of the Crown by pretence of prerogative, without grant of Parliament, for longer time, or in other manner than the same is or shall be granted, is illegal;

• That it is the right of the subjects to petition the king, and all commitments and prosecutions for such petitioning are illegal;

• That the raising or keeping a standing army within the kingdom in time of peace, unless it be with consent of Parliament, is against law;

• That election of members of Parliament ought to be free;

• That the freedom of speech and debates or proceed-

ings in Parliament ought not to be impeached or questioned in any court or place out of Parliament;
• ... And that for redress of all grievances, and for the amending, strengthening and preserving of the laws, Parliaments ought to be held frequently."

C | FROM 'INTRODUCTION TO THE STUDY OF THE LAW OF THE CONSTITUTION', BY A V DICEY (1885; 10TH EDN, 1959 BY E C S WADE)
"The principle of Parliamentary sovereignty means neither more nor less than this, namely that Parliament thus defined has, under the English constitution, the right to make or unmake any law whatever; and, further, that no person or body is recognised by the law of England as having a right to override or set aside the legislation of Parliament..."

"Parliamentary sovereignty is therefore an undoubted legal fact. It is complete both on its positive and on its negative side. Parliament can legally legislate on any topic whatever which, in the judgment of Parliament, is a fit subject for legislation. There is no power which, under the English constitution, can come into rivalry with the legislative sovereignty of Parliament. No one of the limitations alleged to be imposed by law on the absolute authority of Parliament has any real existence, or receives any countenance, either from the statute-book or from the practice of the Courts."

D | FROM 'TREATISE ON THE LAW, PRIVILEGES, PROCEEDINGS AND USAGE OF PARLIAMENT', BY THOMAS ERSKINE MAY (FIRST EDITION, 1844)
"The legislative authority of Parliament extends over the United Kingdom, and all its colonies and foreign possessions; there are no other limits to its power of making laws for the whole empire than those which are incident to all sovereign authority — the willingness of the peo-

ple to obey, or their power to resist. Unlike the legislatures of many other countries, it is bound by no fundamental charter or constitution; but has itself the sole
constitutional right of establishing and altering the laws
and government of the empire."

*E | FROM 'THE ENGLISH CONSTITUTION', BY WALTER
BAGEHOT (1867)*
"The ultimate authority in the English Constitution is a
newly-elected House of Commons."

A KINGDOM DIVIDED, UNITED BY LACK OF CONSTITUTIONAL CLARITY

JAMES CUSICK on the haphazard relationship between the UK's component parts

=

IN LONDON'S Olympic velodrome, seven months before Scotland's 2014 vote on whether to exit or remain part of the United Kingdom, David Cameron struggled to define what was at stake. He called the UK an "intricate tapestry", a 300-year-old collaboration of inter-nation relationships and shared values that had been built "brick by brick".

Leaving aside the political hyperbole and the metaphorical confusion, the Prime Minister was correct in acknowledging there is no single piece of constitutional architecture, no one legal instrument that glues the UK together. Regardless of the emotional allure of the scepter'd isle, the fusion of the UK's constituent parts is, as the historian Linda Colley has pointed out, a product of "constantly refurbishing and reinventing" the core "idea of union."

However, this ever-evolving historia Britanniae does not mean that the Union's story is devoid of points of significant invention.

With England a unified kingdom from the 10th century, and Scotland almost under central control from the 13th, the attraction of a formal conjoining was evident early on. In 1289 the twin treaties of Birgham and Salisbury were almost delivered. Ambassadors from the English king, Edward I, negotiated a deal with a Scottish parliament representing Margaret, the Maid of Norway, who at the age of three had been given the Scottish crown. The plan: Edward's son would marry Margaret and the two kingdoms would unite. The legal backdrop now looks familiar: the Scots would retain what they owned, "separate and divided from England according to its rightful boundaries, free in itself and without subjection." The Scottish Parliament and the national church would remain distinct entities. Britain, great or not, looked like arriving 400 years earlier than it did. Only the death of the young Margaret in Orkney, and later suspicions about the limited independence guarantees offered by the English, saw the plan shredded.

By the time Robert Bruce had seized the Scottish throne, there was still uncertainty over succession, regardless of significant victories over the English such as Bannockburn in 1314. The Declaration of Arbroath in 1320 was intended to address this. Sent to Pope John XXII in Avignon, it used a "language of liberty", as Colley calls it, that resonated beyond its basic purpose. "For, as long as a hundred of us remain alive, never will we on any conditions be subjected to the lordship of the English." If the historian Simon Schama is correct, and "the great theme of British history is the fate of freedom", then the Arbroath document is pivotal.

Wales, once regarded as a problematic principality, came under London's control ahead of Scotland or Ireland. The initial 14th century conquest by Edward I came at some expense, and for the next 200 years was largely seen as an incomplete annexation. The 1536 Act of Union, more corporate raid than union, and another Act seven years later, ended that fragmented colonisation. Wales was declared "for ever from henceforth incorporated, united and annexed to" England. English law and language now ruled and Wales' representative politicians decamped to Westminster. Somewhere in between, the Welsh name Tewdwr became subservient to the English Tudor, although Wales' cultural identity was never mislaid.

Despite the administrative posturing of the Arbroath Abbey document, the fall-out from the succession confrontation between Elizabeth I and the daughter of Scotland's James V and Mary of Guise - better known as Mary Queen of Scots - advanced the elusive Union of Crowns. In 1603 a Scottish king, Mary's son, James VI, became the single sovereign of England and Ireland, Scotland and Wales.

Paintings by Sir Peter Paul Rubens on the ceiling of the Banqueting Hall in Whitehall show the new king, James I, confident in his belief that his unified territory was Dei Gratia, blessed and approved by God. The political reality was different. Scotland and England still had their separate parliaments, and within half a century England was gripped by civil war, James' son Charles was executed (part of Oliver Cromwell's "cruel necessity"), and when monarchy returned the instability continued.

But throughout, as Schama has pointed out, although governance may have seemed perched in a half-way house between tyranny and democracy, there was still parliament, and there was still the law.

The 1689 Bill of Rights in England, and the Claim of Right in Scotland, saw the Edinburgh and London parliaments agree on the crown by-passing James II and going to Prince William of Orange. (Ireland, too, thanks to an earlier 16th-century proclamation and the expansion of English rule, faced, reluctantly, a new era of dominant Protestant authority.) The wider resonance, however, was the principle of parliamentary supremacy: the English and Scottish legislatures, though close on their fundamental beliefs, were still divided on what ever-closer union would mean.

The Act of Settlement in 1701 secured a Protestant monarch for England, an invited Hanoverian. Three years later, with the Scottish treasury suffering melt-down from a failed attempt at establishing a colony in Panama, and amid fears of famine at home, Edinburgh passed the Act of Security, granting Scotland the right to challenge England's choice of successor. This was an effective political threat, which told Westminster to open its colonial trade to struggling Scottish merchants.

It wasn't a zero-sum game: both sides had something to gain. In Whitehall in April 1706 in a location called The Cockpit (where Henry VIIII had once staged cock-fighting), another type of battle began.

At the end of three days of negotiations between appointed commissioners from England and Scotland, where neither side met face-to-face, the Scots were offered terms on what we now call the Union: "England and Scotland be forever united in one kingdom by the name of Great Britain."

The flag design was agreed, as were weights, measures, heritable offices and the numbers of peers and MPs in Westminster. Scotland was offered tax exemptions, and the preservation of its own legal, banking and education systems. The Scottish kirk was also left unchallenged.

Compensation – and, depending on your perspective, bribes – were sent north to those who could influence the union vote in the Scottish parliament. When the draft treaty was published, riots broke out across Scotland. A draft document was burnt by the hangman in the centre on Edinburgh. A month later, however, the Act of Union passed, in January 1707, and two months on the Scottish Parliament adjourned itself.

According to Colley, what was agreed was "flexible

and in many respects only a partial union which explains why it has endured for so long."

Meanwhile, the Union grew. In 1800 and 1801 the Acts of Union, addressing the limitations of the Irish parliament and the emergence of a new generation of nationalists, created the single polity of Great Britain and Ireland (which had hitherto been linked only loosely via the monarchy). This structure endured until the failures of Home Rule in the late 19th century, culminating in the Easter Rising in 1916 and the arrival of the Irish Free State in 1922 – leaving only the six counties of Northern Ireland as part of the Union.

So what will the next chapter of Albion's union and the UK's evolving island story look like? The Scotland Act 1998 devolved primary law-making power back to Scotland, leading to its adjourned parliament reconvening for the first time in 300 years. Wales was also given limited devolution the same year, with its powers further enhanced in the Government of Wales Act 2006.

According to Colley, these devolutionary measures were "insufficiently thought out" and will result only in demands for even greater autonomy.

If there have been game-changing events which confirm this thesis, they include the Scottish Nationalist Party gaining overall control of the Edinburgh parliament; the party's push for the 2014 referendum; and its unprecedented success in May's general election. All point to a fragile rather than a robust Union - whose immediate political future must be in doubt.

As for the constitutional precepts that might influence the future of the union, the uneasy truth is that this still-evolving patchwork of relationships effectively justifies forecasts of both survival and fragmentation. The only certainty is that everything will not remain the same.

OUR UNWRITTEN CONSTITUTION

KEY TEXTS ON THE UNITED KINGDOM

A | FROM THE DECLARATION OF ARBROATH (1320; TRANSLATED BY SIR JAMES FERGUSSON)

" ... outrages without number which he [Edward I] committed against our people, sparing neither age nor sex, religion nor rank, no-one could describe nor fully imagine unless he had seen them with his own eyes.

"But from these countless evils we have been set free ...by our most tireless prince, King and lord, the lord Robert."

"To him, as to the man by whom salvation has been wrought unto our people, we are bound both by his right and by his merits that our freedom may be still maintained, and by him, come what may, we mean to stand."

"Yet if he should give up what he has begun, seeking to make us or our kingdom subject to the King of England or the English, we should exert ourselves at once to drive him out as our enemy and a subverter of his own right and ours, and make some other man who was well able to defend us our King; for, as long as a hundred of us remain alive, never will we on any conditions be subjected to the lordship of the English."

B | FROM Y DEDDFAU CYFREITHIAU YNG NHGYMRU (LAWS IN WALES ACT) 1536 AND 1543

"His Highness therefore of a singular Zeal, Love and Favour that he beareth towards his Subjects of his said Dominion of Wales, minding and intending to reduce them to the perfect Order, Notice and Knowledge of his Laws of this Realm, and utterly to extirp all and singular the sinister Usages and Customs differing from the same, and to bring the said Subjects of this his Realm, and of his said Dominion of Wales, to an amicable Concord and Unity..."

"That his said Country or Dominion of Wales shall be, stand and continue for ever from henceforth incorporated, united and annexed to and with this his Realm of England;"

C | FROM THE UNION WITH ENGLAND ACT 1707
"That the Two Kingdoms of Scotland and England shall ... hereof and forever after be United into One Kingdom by the Name of Great Britain And that the Ensigns Armorial of the said United Kingdom be such as Her Majesty shall appoint and the Crosses of St Andrew and St George be conjoined in such manner as Her Majesty shall think fit and used in all Flags Banners Standards and Ensigns both at Sea and Land."

"That the United Kingdom of Great Britain be Represented by one and the same Parliament to be stiled the Parliament of Great Britain."

"That all the Subjects of the United Kingdom of Great Britain shall from and after the Union have full Freedom and Intercourse of Trade and Navigation to and from any port or place within the said United Kingdom and the Dominions and Plantations thereunto belonging..."

"That the Court of Session or Colledge of Justice do after the Union and notwithstanding thereof remain in all time coming within Scotland as it is now constituted by the Laws of that Kingdom."

D | FROM THE UNION WITH IRELAND ACT 1800
"That Great Britain and Ireland shall upon Jan. 1, 1801, be united into one kingdom; and that the titles appertaining to the crown, &c. shall be such as his Majesty shall be pleased to appoint."

"That the United Kingdom be represented in one Parliament."

"That such Act as shall be passed in Ireland to regu-
late the mode of summoning and returning the lords
and commoners to serve in the united Parliament of the
United Kingdom, shall be considered as part of the treaty of union."

E | FROM THE SCOTLAND ACT 1998
"There shall be a Scottish Parliament."

AN INVISIBLE PILLAR, SHROUDED IN MYSTERY AND TRADITION

CAHAL MILMO considers the ill-defined but inescapable role of the monarch

=

LIKE HIS father before him and every other member of the House of Windsor with an expectation of becoming monarch, the young Prince George will one day be asked to ponder the musings of the son of a Somerset banker on the peculiar institution he is ordained to eventually lead.

In 1867, Walter Bagehot, the great essayist and long-serving editor of The Economist, suggested in his work The English Constitution that there was no point in explaining the monarchy as a rational part of British society. It has been a set text for little kings and queens in waiting ever since.

Bagehot observed that the role served by the Sovereign since leaving behind the era when the day job consisted of donning armour and eviscerating rivals was to float above the filthy business of wielding power and instead embody a sense of "mystery" – a unifying figurehead gifted by history and surrounded by ritual.

He wrote: "The mystic reverence, the religious allegiance, which are essential to a true monarchy, are imaginative sentiments that no legislature can manufacture in any people. You might as well adopt a father as make a monarchy."

The Victorian polemicist was writing for an age when the monarch was also an empress and Britain a superpower. But he put his finger on a defining characteristic of royalty in the United Kingdom as it made the transition to its modern status as the cherry on the very British cake of constitutional monarchy: that of survival by persuading Britons of its utility as much as its regality.

Bagehot suggested that this compact involved the monarch imparting a sort of wisdom of the age through a triumvirate of residual "rights". The Sovereign, he wrote, enjoyed "the right to be consulted, the right to encourage, the right to warn", and in exercising these rights would win the affection of his or her subjects.

In Britain's genteel pyramid of power, the monarch has swapped political power for the expectation of consultation by those – namely the Prime Minister and the Prime Minister's Cabinet – who exercise that power on his or her behalf.

In more recent years, however, this role has been presented differently. The Royal Household has created a dual-purpose monarch who not only wears the crown but is also a fount of "soft power", a bulwark against the more venal forces in modern life. Alongside the Queen's duties as Head of State (opening Parliament, meeting Prime Ministers, making overseas visits), Britain now has a "Head of Nation".

As the Official Website of the British Monarchy puts it: "As 'Head of Nation', The Queen's role is less formal, but no less important for the social and cultural functions it fulfills.

"These include: providing a focus for national identity, unity and pride; giving a sense of stability and continuity; recognising success, achievement and excellence; and supporting service to others."

It is an eccentrically British feature of the unwritten constitution that the overarching philosophy of one of its cornerstones (a head of state elevated by birth rather than merit) is to be found not in ancient manuscripts but in the writings of a motley crew of journalists and screenwriters. Just as Prince George, like his father, grandfather and great-grandmother before him, will pore over Bagehot for guidance, so too will he owe the latest definition of royalty's constitutional purpose to a leading comedy writer.

Sir Antony Jay, whose gifts to the nation include co-creating Yes, Prime Minister, is credited with first outlining the twin notions of Head of State and Head of Nation in a book published alongside his defining 1990s documentary on the role of the Queen, Elizabeth R. The monarch's duties, he wrote, "can be done well, or adequately, or badly, or not done at all. They are the ones concerned with behaviour, values and standards; the ones which earn the respect, loyalty and pride of the people."

It is no accident that, for the past 150 years or so, definitions of the monarch's constitutional role have been borrowed magpie-like from diviners of popular sentiment such as comedians and hacks. For without the common touch, an institution that depends on securing both the deference and the affection of its subjects runs the risk of losing their consent. And, if nothing else, monarchy in Britain is a game of consent.

Since Charles I paid the ultimate price for insisting on clinging on to the powers of an absolute monarch when his subjects were no longer content to grant them, British sovereigns have shown with varying degrees of deftness an ability to cede power and yet remain the seat of all authority.

This is done by dint of "royal prerogative" – a slightly slippery notion defined by the constitutional expert Albert Dicey as the rump of the Crown's "original authority" that remains outside Parliament's gift but is in practice surrendered to the Government of the day.

The present Queen therefore governs, but only according to the rules or conventions laid down by an elected Parliament and its Government. It is only through Elizabeth II's signature or assent that laws come into existence – but by way of a constitutional quid pro quo she only signs what her ministers ask her to.

This is the result of 300 years or so of progressive clipping of royal wings through legislation, beginning with the 1689 Bill of Rights, which laid out basic civil rights and established the supremacy of Parliament in passing laws, as well as stripping the monarch of the power to maintain an army in peacetime without MPs' consent.

The Act of Settlement 12 years later, which continues to ensure that no Catholic can sit on the throne and only recently saw its provision for male primogeniture expunged from the statute book, also further restricted the powers of the Crown. Among its clauses was a provision that judges held office on the basis of their own good conduct rather than at the direct say-so of the Sovereign, thereby establishing the independence of the judiciary.

This gradual ceding of power in return for retaining influence has allowed the monarchy to defeat the republican logic which was outlined by Anglo-American revolutionary Thomas Paine in 1776 (and which has resulted in most other liberal democracies functioning without a royal head of state). In his pamphlet Common Sense, Paine wrote: "There is something exceedingly ridiculous in the composition of Monarchy. One of the strongest natural proofs of the folly of the hereditary right in kings is that nature disapproves it, otherwise she would not so frequently turn it into ridicule by giving mankind an ass for a lion."

At least since Bagehot, the retort of the system to

such criticism (which even the great Victorian apologist for monarchy admitted had some rational basis) has been that a royal head of state creates a unifying rather than a divisive figurehead.

Vernon Bogdanor, the eminent constitutional expert, wrote that heredity "settles beyond argument the crucial argument of who is to be head of state, and places the position beyond political competition".

Britons would broadly seem to agree – support for a republic in the UK has consistently bumped along at between 15 and 25 per cent in polls for several decades. Support for the monarchy stood at nearly 80 per cent for the Queen's Diamond Jubilee in 2012.

Yet a monarchy that exists by consent is nonetheless fragile and not without inconsistencies. Although the Queen has no direct political power (and has been punctilious in avoiding any hint of party allegiance), the laws of the land none the less mean she theoretically remains able to exercise the royal prerogative contrary to the advice of her prime minister or the Cabinet.

As such, she has the power to prorogue or close a Parliamentary session at her own will, to appoint whomsoever she pleases as Prime Minister and even refuse royal assent to a bill (though the last time this happened was in in 1704 under Queen Anne). It is only the 1,000-year-old web of convention and precedent – and Her Majesty's personal restraint – which means such a scenario does not occur.

The hotch-potch nature of the constitution is shown by the fact that the Sovereign retains all manner of unusual rights secured by her forebears and never claimed back. For example, she can can to this day by law demand the surrender of any sturgeon caught or landed in British waters, or force men into the Royal Navy or dig for salpetre.

Britain's most eminent and legal minds have long struggled to define the royal prerogative and indeed which powers it continues to confer on both the monarch and her ministers. Attempts to bring at least the majority of these powers under Parliamentary control by putting them on the statute book have long been mooted and equally long postponed because to do so would leave MPs and peers with no time to debate the more pressing matter of the legislation of the day.

The result is that there is little prospect of the monarchy, with all its carefully choreographed mystique of ritual and ancient influence, being unstitched from the workings of the British state.

It is, at least, a feat of endurance admired the world over. When King Farouk of Egypt was removed from his throne in 1952 he observed that "soon there will be only five kings left". The list consisted of the kings of spades, diamonds, hearts and clubs – and the King of England.

OUR UNWRITTEN CONSTITUTION

KEY TEXTS ON THE MONARCHY

A | FROM THE BILL OF RIGHTS (1689)

"The... Lords Spiritual and Temporal and Commons... declare:
• That the pretended power of suspending the laws or the execution of laws by regal authority without consent of Parliament is illegal;
• That the pretended power of dispensing with laws or the execution of laws by regal authority, as it hath been assumed and exercised of late, is illegal;
• That the commission for erecting the late Court of Commissioners for Ecclesiastical Causes, and all other commissions and courts of like nature, are illegal and pernicious;
• That levying money for or to the use of the Crown by pretence of prerogative, without grant of Parliament, for longer time, or in other manner than the same is or shall be granted, is illegal."

B | FROM 'THE ENGLISH CONSTITUTION' BY WALTER BAGEHOT (1867)

"The sovereign has, under a constitutional monarchy such as ours, three rights – the right to be consulted, the right to encourage, the right to warn. And a king of great sense and sagacity would want no others. He would find that his having no others would enable him to use these with singular effect..."

C | FROM 'COMMENTARIES ON THE LAWS OF ENGLAND', BY SIR WILLIAM BLACKSTONE (1765)

"By the word prerogative we usually understand that special pre-eminence which the King hath, over and above all other persons, and out of the ordinary course of common law, in right of his regal dignity ... it can only be applied to those rights and capacities which the King enjoys alone, in contradiction to others, and not to those which he enjoys in common with any of his subjects."

D | FROM A V DICEY, 'INTRODUCTION TO THE STUDY OF THE LAW OF THE CONSTITUTION' (10TH EDITION, 1959)

"The prerogative is the name of the remaining portion of the Crown's original authority ... Every act which the executive government can lawfully do without the authority of an Act of Parliament is done in virtue of the prerogative."

E | FROM 'THE GOVERNANCE OF BRITAIN: REVIEW OF THE EXECUTIVE ROYAL PREROGATIVE POWERS (FINAL REPORT)', BY THE MINISTRY OF JUSTICE (2009)

This review includes this summary of the Crown or Monarch's constitutional or personal prerogatives:

"Appointment and removal of Ministers; appointment of Prime Minister ; power to dismiss government; power to summon, prorogue and dissolve Parliament; assent to legislation; the appointment of privy counsellors; granting of honours, decorations, arms and regulating matters of precedence; Queen's honours – Order of the Garter, Order of the Thistle, Royal Victorian Order and the Order of Merit; a power to appoint judges in a residual category of posts which are not statutory and other holders of public office where that office is non-statutory; a power to legislate under the prerogative by Order in Council or by letters patent in a few residual areas, such as Orders in Council for British Overseas Territories; grant of special leave to appeal from certain non-UK courts to the Privy Council; may require the personal services of subjects in case of imminent danger; grant of civic honours and civic dignities; grant of approval for certain uses of Royal names and titles..."

The report also lists a number of "archaic prerogative powers", while conceding that "it is unclear whether some of these... continue to exist". They include: "guardianship of infants and those suffering certain mental disorders; right to bona vacantia; right to sturgeon, (wild and unmarked) swans and whales as casual revenue; right to wreck as casual revenue; right to construct and supervise harbours; by prerogative right the Crown is prima facie the owner of all land covered by the narrow seas adjoining the coast... ; right to waifs & strays; right to impress men into the Royal Navy; right to mint coinage; right to mine precious metals (Royal Mines); also to dig for saltpetre..."

A UNION TOO FAR? THE ISSUE THAT STRAINS SOVEREIGNTY TO THE LIMITS

OLIVER WRIGHT examines the UK's troubled relationship with the EU

=

IF YOU look back over the last 40 years, it is hard to think of any political issue or debate that has transcended generations and is still as "live" and important today as it was then. Unilateral disarmament, the fate of the mining industry, or the stark ideological differences between labour and capital that divided the country in the 1970s and 1980s: all these have come and gone; or, at least, have dwindled into some kind of broad political consensus that reflects changing reality.

But there is one notable exception: Europe, and the vexed question of what exactly what we want our relationship with our closest neighbours to be.

This month is the 40th anniversary of the last time the UK held a referendum on our country's membership of what was then the European Economic Community. David Cameron cites this time gap as a reason for the British people to have another say on the subject. Yet in fact it says something different. It says that, at a profound level, we haven't moved on. A "no" campaign leaflet from that time offers the risk to jobs and sovereignty as reasons to pull out of the Common Market – in short, not especially different from today.

So how exactly did this troubled relationship come about? How did it evolve? And how much power does it now exert over our everyday lives?

The European Union started its life not long after the Second World War as organisation called the European Steel and Coal Community. Ostensibly its aim was to create a common market for French and German coal and steel production under a "joint authority" established by both countries. But steel and coal are weapons of war, and the Treaty of Paris (1951), which gave birth to the ESCC, was actually about binding the French and West German economies together in such a way that war would be, if not impossible, at least much more difficult.

In a way that central tenet has never entirely disappeared from purpose of the ESCC's successor bodies. Continental leaders, particularly in France and Germany, see the European Project in quite simple terms: that it is only through consensual politics and ever closer union that you can permanently prevent one power from dominating Europe by force again. We in Britain have never quite seen it that way – but then we were never occupied.

If the Treaty of Paris was the foundation stone of what we now know as the European Union it was the 1957 Treaty of Rome that gave birth to the European institutions as we know them today. In addition to creating a customs union between its six original signatories (Belgium, France, Luxembourg, Italy, the Netherlands and West Germany), this also resulted in the old "joint authority" of the ESCC becoming an embryonic European Commission, while a small democratic mandate was provided by Common Assembly that later became the European Parliament.

Britain at this stage was still an outside the club – although we were members of the quite separate Council of Europe (founded in 1950) and were signed up to the European Convention on Human Rights (which came into effect in 1953). It wasn't until 1961 that the UK, along with Denmark, Ireland, Norway, officially applied to become a member of what was then the European Economic Community (EEC).

But it was not to be. The French President Charles de Gaulle, concerned that British membership would weaken the French voice within the EEC and that close Anglo-American relations would lead to the United States increasing its influence in Europe, vetoed the move –adding the memorable justification: "l'Angleterre, ce n'est plus grand chose" ("England is not much any more").

This was how things remained for much of the 1960s until President de Gaulle left the scene and Britain resubmitted its application for membership. Negotiations began in 1970 under the Conservative (and pro-European) government of Edward Heath, and Britain officially acceded to the Community in January 1973.

Even then, however, our relationship with Europe was a thorny political issue. The Labour Party, in particular, was divided on the issue, and Harold Wilson was forced to include a pledge for an in/out referendum in his 1974 election manifesto.

When his party won power, the referendum – on the question "Do you think the United Kingdom should remain part of the European Community (the Common Market)?" – duly took place: the first nationwide plebiscite to be held in the UK during the 20th century. Wilson backed a "yes" vote – as did Margaret Thatcher, who was pictured wearing a top featuring the flags of all the European countries on it. The vote was convincingly won by the "yes" side, by 67 to 32 per cent.

There was then a period of relative quiet on the European controversy front, lasting for the rest of the

1970s and much of the 1980s – the only exception being 1985, when the Schengen Agreement led to the creation of open borders without passport controls between most member states apart from the UK.

This calm was in large part due to Mrs Thatcher's success in 1984 in securing a rebate in funds paid by Britain to the EEC to make up for the high proportion of spending that went on the Common Agricultural Policy (which disproportionately benefited France).

But it all flared up again in the early 1990s. This time, the bone of contention was Britain's ratification of the Maastricht Treaty (1992), which turned the EEC into the European Union. Maastricht effectively set the EU on the path to ever closer political and monitory union and was vociferously opposed by the Conservative right when the bill to ratify the agreement went through the House of Commons.

John Major negotiated several important opt-outs – including from the single currency and social chapter on workers' pay and health and safety – but many in his party could never accept the basic principle of the treaty: that the European Union should gradually replace the nation state as the ultimate source of political power in Europe.

These mainly Tory divisions on Europe were a large extent swept away, along with the party, when Tony Blair won his landslide victory in 1997. Questions about sovereignty were not so much resolved as brushed aside – or, in practical terms, eroded by time. People grew used to the increased impact of the EU on British life – while European considerations became increasingly embedded in, for example, legal precedent. Mr Blair, meanwhile, was determined to put Britain's relationship with the EU on a better footing – and was also determined to reform the EU itself.

Oddly, given the flavour of much of the current British debate about Europe, it was the UK that was the most enthusiastic proponent of EU enlargement, which led to accession of the former Eastern bloc countries in 2004 and 2007. We pushed enlargement then because we believed this would dilute the EU's Franco-German axis and that country's such as Poland would be more sympathetic to the British perspective. What was not anticipated was the influx of labour which, while welcome in the good times, quickly turned toxic following the financial crisis of 2008.

And so here we are today: with another EU referendum looming and the country still divided over what we want our relationship to be.

When the moment comes, we will probably vote to stay in, just as we did in 1975.

But – as in 1975 – that is very unlikely to be the end of the matter.

OUR UNWRITTEN CONSTITUTION

KEY TEXTS ON EUROPE

A | FROM THE EUROPEAN COMMUNITIES ACT 1972 (SECTION 2:1; AMENDED 2008)

"All such rights, powers, liabilities, obligations and restrictions from time to time created or arising by or under the Treaties, and all such remedies and procedures from time to time provided for by or under the Treaties, as in accordance with the Treaties are without further enactment to be given legal effect or used in the United Kingdom, shall be recognised and available in law, and be enforced, allowed and followed accordingly..."

B | FROM "TREATISE ON THE LAW, PRIVILEGES, PROCEEDINGS AND USAGE OF PARLIAMENT", ORIGINALLY BY THOMAS ERSKINE MAY BUT SUBSEQUENTLY UPDATED (24TH EDITION, 2011)

"Accession of the United Kingdom to membership of the European Communities (now the European Union) on 1 January 1973 qualified the exclusive legislative authority of the United Kingdom Parliament ... Although the primary obligations created by [section 2 of the European Communities Act 1972] are susceptible of amendment by Parliament, by virtue of the doctrine of the supremacy of Parliament, the courts have on a number of occasions had to consider the relative priority of United Kingdom statute law and law which has effect by virtue of the Treaties and the Act of 1972. It has been decided that European law takes priority over inconsistent United Kingdom law, not because the former supplants the latter, but because European law is part of United Kingdom law."

C | THE MAASTRICHT TREATY (1992)

The signatories declared themselves "resolved to establish a citizenship common to nationals of their countries", "resolved to implement a common foreign and security policy" and "resolved to continue the process of creating an ever closer union among the peoples of Europe"; and declared that they had "decided to establish a European Union."

D | FROM THE HUMAN RIGHTS ACT (1998), SECTIONS 3 AND 6 (1) (REFERRING TO THE EUROPEAN CONVENTION ON HUMAN RIGHTS (1950), WHICH ESTABLISHED THE EUROPEAN COURT OF HUMAN RIGHTS IN STRASBOURG)

"So far as it is possible to do so, primary legislation and subordinate legislation must be read and given effect in a way which is compatible with the Convention rights. This... does not affect the validity, continuing operation or enforcement of any incompatible primary legislation; and does not affect the validity, continuing operation or enforcement of any incompatible subordinate legislation if (disregarding any possibility of revocation) primary legislation prevents removal of the incompatibility..."

"It is unlawful for a public authority to act in a way which is incompatible with a Convention right."

E | FROM LORD HOFFMANN'S JUDGMENT IN R (SIMMS) V HOME SECRETARY (1999)

"Parliamentary sovereignty means that Parliament can, if it chooses, legislate contrary to fundamental principles of human rights. The Human Rights Act 1998 will not detract from this power. The constraints upon its exercise by Parliament are ultimately political, not legal. But the principle of legality means that Parliament must squarely confront what it is doing and accept the political cost. Fundamental rights cannot be overridden by general or ambiguous words. .. In the absence of express language or necessary implication to the contrary, the courts therefore presume that even the most general words were intended to be subject to the basic rights of the individual. In this way the courts of the United Kingdom, though acknowledging the sovereignty of Parliament, apply principles of constitutionality little different from those which exist in countries where the power of the legislature is expressly limited by a constitutional document".

F | FROM LORD HOPE OF CRAIGHEAD'S JUDGMENT IN R (JACKSON) V ATTORNEY-GENERAL (2006)

"Our constitution is dominated by the sovereignty of Parliament. But Parliamentary sovereignty is no longer, if it ever was, absolute... Step by step, gradually but surely, the English principle of the absolute legislative sovereignty of Parliament which Dicey derived from Coke and Blackstone is being qualified."

G | FROM THE CABINET MANUAL (2011) (SECTION 9, PARAGRAPHS 15-18)

"The UK is obliged to ensure that its national laws and measures are compliant with EU law..."

"If the UK fails to implement its obligations fully, it is liable to face legal proceedings (known as infraction proceedings) brought by the European Commission before the Court of Justice of the European Union.

"Article 46 of the European Convention on Human Rights obliges the UK to implement judgments made against it by the European Court of Human Rights... Both individual and general measures must be completed to the satisfaction of the Committee of Ministers of the Council of Europe, which can take steps against the UK if it decides that a judgment is not being properly implemented."

"Reflecting the will of the citizens and States of Europe to build a common future, this Constitution establishes the European Union, on which the Member States confer competences to attain objectives they have in common..."

"The Member States shall take any appropriate measure, general or particular, to ensure fulfilment of the obligations arising out of the Constitution or resulting from the acts of the institutions of the Union."

"The Member States shall facilitate the achievement of the Union's tasks and refrain from any measure which could jeopardise the attainment of the Union's objectives."

"The Constitution and law adopted by the institutions of the Union in exercising competences conferred on it shall have primacy over the law of the Member States."

12355889R00037

Printed in Great Britain
by Amazon.co.uk, Ltd.,
Marston Gate.